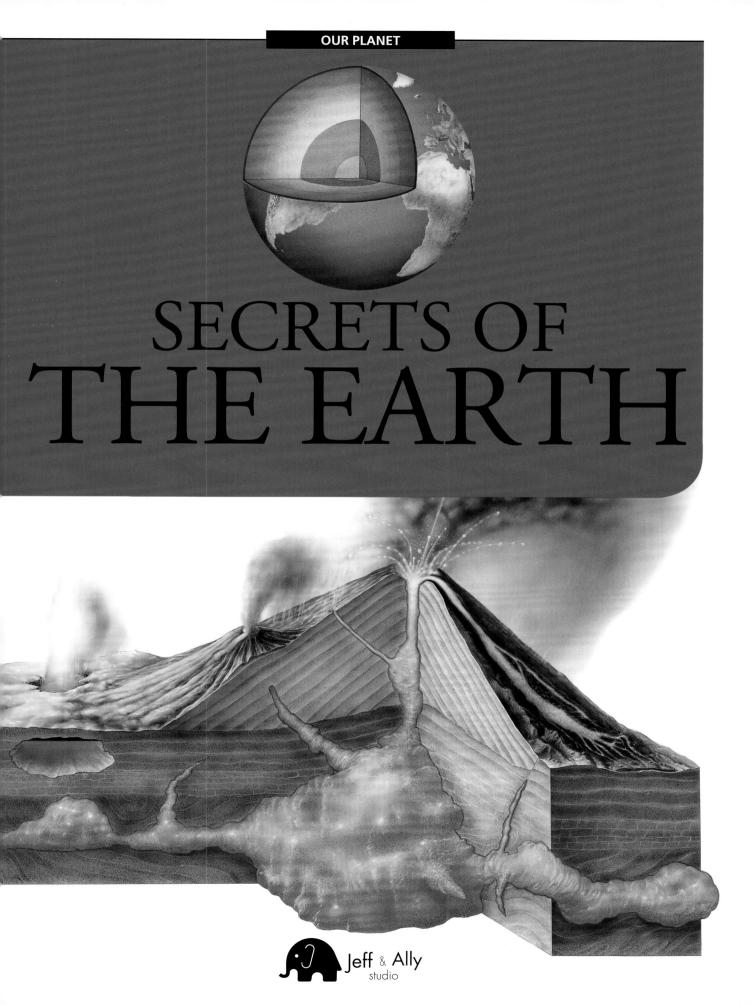

SECRETS OF
THE EARTH

Jeff & Ally studio

SECRETS OF THE EARTH
- Augmented Reality

Original title of the book in Spanish:
SECRETOS DE LA TIERRA
- Augmented Reality

Project: Parramón Paidotribo

Texts: Eduardo Banqueri

Illustrations: Estudio Marcel Socías

Design: Estudi Toni Inglés (Alba Marco)

© Copyright 2016 Parramon Paidotribo-
World Rights

English Translation: Dominic Hayes
English edition: © 2016 by Design Media
Publishing (UK) Limited
This edition is published in April 2016

Design Media Publishing (UK) Limited
Chase Business Centre
39-41 Chase Side
London
N14 5BP

www.designmediauk.com
E-mail: info@designmediauk.com

ISBN: 978-1-910596-60-9

Printed in China

OUR HOME IN THE UNIVERSE

This book is intended for young readers who are especially interested in knowledge of the Earth. Geology is the science concerned with the study of the planet. It is an extraordinarily interesting field since it encompasses all the issues related to our planet: its origin, composition, structure, its past and future, its current processes, evolution and, finally, the many phenomena that have taken and are taking place on it.

In these pages, we do not claim that this book is a complete reference work; instead, we have selected topics that show that the Earth is a living planet, with both an interior dynamic (volcanoes, earthquakes, movements of tectonic plates, formation of igneous and metamorphic rocks, etc.) and an exterior one (weathering, erosion, transportation of materials, sedimentation, formation of sedimentary rocks, etc.). The explanation of the Earth's history follows the actual sequence of events. For this reason, it starts with an outline of the Earth's origin, before continuing with an examination of its structure and composition. Next, we focus on the planet's internal dynamic and its consequences (tectonic plates, volcanoes, etc.) and following that we look at different processes of external activity (the action of underground aquifers, of glaciers, and of oceans). Finally, we have included a chapter dedicated to the interpretation of topographical maps, a fundamental tool for the study and understanding of the shape of the Earth's surface.

As is the case with humanity itself, it is not possible to understand the present if the past is unknown. For this reason, the most important events in the evolution of our planet are explained in the introduction, supplemented with a table of geological periods at the back of the book.

A PLANET WITH A HISTORY BEHIND IT

The Earth occupies a privileged position within the Solar System, since it is located at the precise distance from the Sun needed to get the right amount of sunlight.

SUITABLE FOR LIFE

The Earth is the third closest planet to the Sun, at a distance of around 150 million kilometres. It is the biggest of the inner Solar System planets and fifth largest of the nine principal worlds orbiting the Sun. These mean that it can maintain a gaseous layer, an atmosphere that scatters light and absorbs heat, so that the Earth does not get too hot by day and too cold by night. Seventy per cent of the Earth's surface is covered in water, which also helps to regulate its temperature. The water that evaporates forms clouds and falls in the shape of rain or snow, forming rivers and lakes.

The Earth is the only heavenly body known where life exists, where there is an atmosphere with oxygen and liquid water on its surface, although this has not always been the case.

When it comes to addressing the history of our planet we encounter the same problem as we do with the history of humanity: there is a long period of time about which we know nothing. This period is known as the Cryptozoic.

THE CRYPTOZOIC EON

This is the oldest, longest and most mysterious part of the Earth's evolution. Cryptozoic means 'hidden life', since the first living organisms appeared at the end of this period, although we have hardly any traces of them. This period is also known as the Precambrian and covers the first 3.9 billion years of the Earth's history.

The Precambrian or Cryptozoic is subdivided into three phases:

• **Pre-Archean or Hadean Eon** (4.5 billion - 3.8 billion years ago). It includes the first moments of the formation of the planetary ball of rock and the period of intense meteor bombardment. At the

During its first few million years of existence, the Earth was in an incandescent state and was subjected to an intense meteor bombardment.

The Archean period was one of great volcanic activity. Gases expelled by eruptions eventually formed part of the atmosphere and water vapour condensed, giving rise to intense rains that produced the Earth's seas and oceans.

beginning, our planet was in a state of fusion and surrounded by an atmosphere made up of huge masses of water vapour and un-breathable gases.

• **Archean Eon** (3.8 billion - 2.5 billion years ago). In this phase the Earth's crust was sufficiently established and had cooled down enough for a primitive atmosphere to exist. It is a time of great volcanic activity and, because of this, vast quantities of magma rise to the surface of the planet, becoming part of the crust as it cools.

• **Proterozoic** (2.5 billion - 570 million years ago). During this period, the first organisms capable of metabolising oxygen and the first multicellular eukaryotes (bacteria and photosynthetic green algae) appear. It is during this period that the primitive atmosphere transforms into one rich in oxygen, which starting with these primordial organisms permits the diversification and evolution of the majority of the groups of invertebrates without a rigid skeleton.

THE PHANEROZOIC

This term signifies 'evident life'. It began some 570 million years ago with an explosion of life, which later extended and diversified across every ocean. In this period, events occur that culminate in the current layout of continents and oceans, and the evolution of living things whose end point is the apparition and development of Man. The Phanerozoic period is divided into three phases: the Paleozoic era (from 570 million to 225 million years ago); the Mesozoic era (from 225 million to 65 million years ago) and the Cenozoic era (from 65 million years ago to the present day, including the Quaternary period, in which Man appears).

A huge diversification of living species took place in the Proterozoic period. These were all marine invertebrates without rigid skeletons, and for this reason the fossil record contains hardly any traces of them.

• **Paleozoic.** Two significant orogenies, the Caledonian and Hercynian, happened during this period, with corresponding fractures and collisions of continents and the subsequent formation of mountain ranges. It has also been determined that there were two long ice ages, interspersed with warmer phases, in which coral formations extended widely. As regards the development of life, the continents were first colonised by plants and arthropods and later by (amphibian) vertebrates.

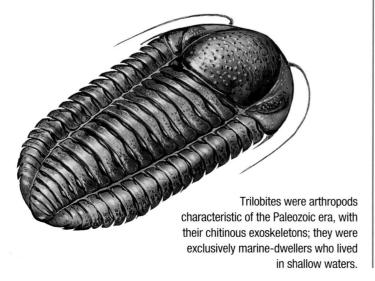

Trilobites were arthropods characteristic of the Paleozoic era, with their chitinous exoskeletons; they were exclusively marine-dwellers who lived in shallow waters.

In the Mesozoic period, reptiles lived in every ecosystem and dominated life on the planet for nearly 200 million years. They became extinct at the end of the period and mammals took their place.

• **The Mesozoic.** During this period, the continents that made up Pangaea gradually separated, and no globally significant orogeny took place. In the beginning, the climate was one of extremes, but it grew milder to become warm and wet for the rest of the period, although at the end there were fresh ice ages. Colonisation of the continents by living things is completed during this era; reptiles develop at an extraordinary rate and mammals and birds appear. The first flowering plants also come into existence. Mass extinctions (of the dinosaurs) occur at the end of the Mesozoic period.

• **The Cenozoic.** This period, the name of which means 'new animals' in Greek, began 65 million years ago and comprises the Tertiary (from 65 to 2.5 million years ago), and the Quaternary (from 2.5 million years ago to the present day). Continents acquire their current profiles during this era. The

The shifting of the tectonic plates, and the consequent collisions between them over the last few million years, have given rise to the great mountain ranges and defined the boundaries of the present era's continents.

proliferation of mammals, which replace reptiles, is another characteristic of this period, and in the middle of the Cenozoic, about 30 million years ago, the first primates with prehensile paws appear, an order of mammals to which belong the various groups of apes and Man himself, although hominids themselves do not emerge until the end of the era, during the Quaternary period.

There is renewed tectonic activity during this period and once again the Earth experiences extreme conditions with four ice ages. In present times, the Earth is still transforming itself. The Earth's crust is fracturing into fifteen enormous plates that create and destroy themselves constantly at their margins and are perennially on the move. As a result, Africa will have divided itself into two within 150 million years and one of these sections will have drifted northwards and joined together with Europe. Antarctica will have united with Australia, and California will have drifted north until it crashes into Alaska.

The first hominids appeared at the end of the Tertiary period, but it will not be until very recent times, towards the end of the last ice age (40,000 years ago), that Homo Sapiens appears on the Earth.

A SLOW BUT THOROUGH JOB

The Earth came into existence 4.6 billion years ago out of a cloud of gas and cosmic dust that made up the nebula the solar system. At the beginning it was a ball of semi-molten white-hot matter. The heaviest elements fell towards the centre to form the metallic core; the lightest rose to the surface and created the rocky mantel and the crust. Over the course of millions of years, the planet cooled, the surface solidified and the atmosphere and the oceans formed.

1 Cloud of gas and dust

2 The Sun's formation
A cloud of gas and dust coalesced to form the Sun 4.6 billion years ago

3 The planets' formation
Other parts of the gas and dust cloud condensed into solid chunks of ice and rock that came together, which gave rise to the planets

4 Radioactivity
The rocks' radioactivity meant that, to begin with, the newly born Earth melted

5 The core's formation
Iron and nickel sank to form the Earth's core, while an ocean of molten rock lay on the surface

6 Great volcanic activity
Thanks to this, the crust grew thicker and the atmosphere was enriched with gases

7 Formation of the atmosphere and oceans
Gases from volcanic eruptions started to create the atmosphere and water vapour condensed, producing the oceans

8 3.5 billion years ago
Most of the crust had formed, but the continents looked very different to now

9 The Present
The crust has broken into enormous plates that create and destroy themselves constantly at their margins

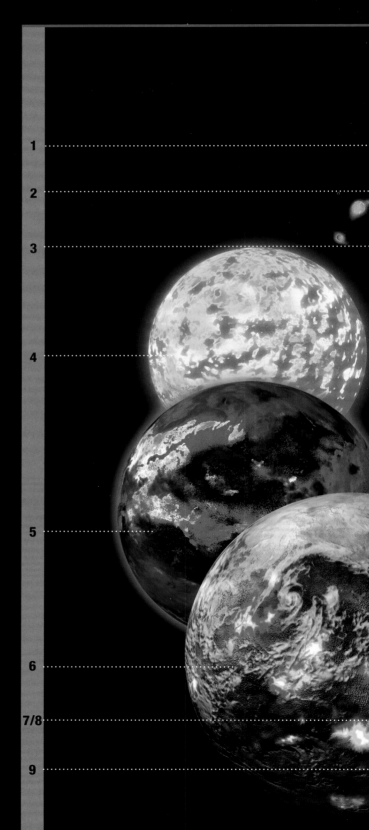

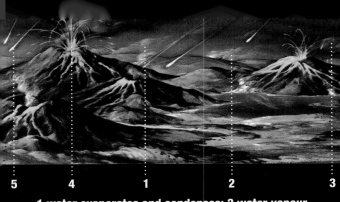

1 water evaporates and condenses; 2 water vapour
condensation; 3 heavy rains and electrical storms;
4 expulsion of magma and gases; 5 meteor showers

The primeval crust

As the crust solidified, water vapour started to
condense and fall in the form of rain, creating the
first oceans. Intense volcanic activity produced
sufficient water vapour to form the primeval
atmosphere.

THE PRIMEVAL ATMOSPHERE

Was composed of methane (CH_4), ammonia
(NH_3), hydrogen sulphide (SH_2), carbon dioxide
(CO_2) and water vapour. Hydrogen and helium
escaped into space and oxygen appeared millions
of years later, when the first photosynthetic
organisms emerged.

CONSEQUENCES OF OUR PLANET'S MOVEMENT

The Sun, and the Earth's movement around it, is the main cause of meteorological and climatic variations. Our planet is endowed with two main astronomic movements: rotation and revolution. These movements give rise to the seasons of the year, the passage of days and nights and the consequent differences of temperature across the planet, producing all the meteorological phenomena that we know.

1 orbit
As it revolves around the Sun, the Earth's orbit is elliptical; it takes slightly more than 365 days to complete

2 rotational movement
Is the Earth's movement around itself on an imaginary axis; it takes 24 hours to complete a turn from west to east

3 winter solstice
Takes place from 21st to 22nd of December; the Sun's rays attain their maximum inclination with respect to the Earth's axis, so that as the North Pole reaches its furthest distance from the Sun, winter begins in the northern hemisphere, and summer starts in the southern hemisphere

THE DISTANCE TO THE SUN CHANGES

Due to the fact that the Earth's orbit around the Sun is elliptical, the distance between the two varies according to the time of year. The point when we are closest to star (in January), at 147.7 million kilometres, is called the perihelion; the point when furthest away (in July), at 152.2 million kilometres, is called the aphelion.

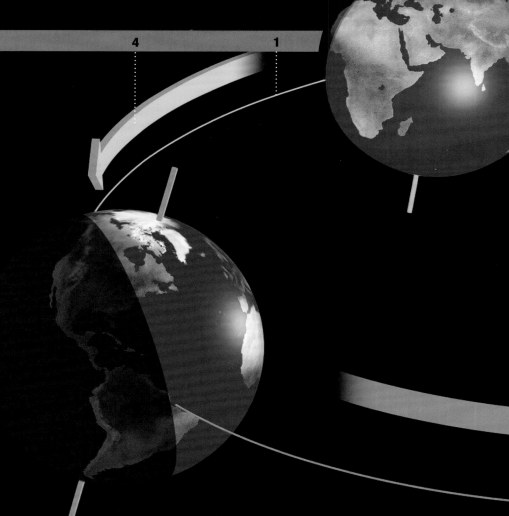

In order to determine the position of a spot on the Earth, a series of imaginary rings parallel to the Equator (called parallels), and a series of circles perpendicular to the rings that converge on the poles (known as meridians), are plotted.

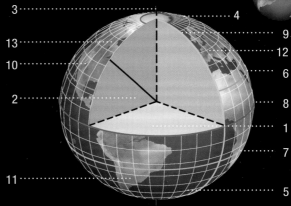

4 summer solstice
Happens on the 21st-22nd of June; the North Pole is at its closest to the Sun, marking the start of summer in the northern hemisphere and winter in the south.

5 spring equinox
Occurs from the 20th to the 21st of March; the sun's rays fall perpendicularly over the Equator, so that the quantity of surface area illuminated is the same in both hemispheres. Day and night are the same lengths. Spring starts in the northern hemisphere and autumn in the south.

6 autumn equinox
Occurs from 22nd to 23rd of September; the Sun's rays fall perpendicularly on the Equator, so the illuminated surface is the same in both hemispheres. Day and night are of equal length; it is the start of autumn in the northern hemisphere and spring in the south.

7 axis of rotation
This is the imaginary axis around which the Earth orbits itself; this axis is not perpendicular to the elliptic, but over the course of the orbit around the Sun it occupies four positions that define the seasons of the year; spring, summer, autumn, winter.

1 longitude
Is the angle measured along the Earth's Equator, between a reference meridium (the Greenwich meridium) and the meridian of the location in question.

2 latitude
The angle determined along the meridian between a terrestrial location and the reference parallel (the Equator).

3 Polar axis
4 Arctic Polar Circle
5 Antarctic Polar Circle
6 Tropic of Cancer
7 Tropic of Capricorn
8 Equator
9 Greenwich meridian
10 Northern hemisphere
11 Southern hemisphere
12 East meridians
13 meridianos oeste

The system of geographic coordinates

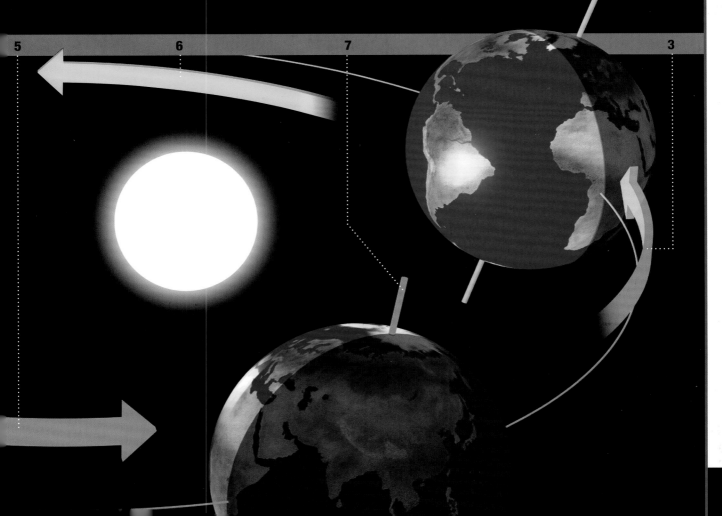

A JOURNEY TO THE CENTRE OF THE EARTH

Studies of changes of direction and speed of seismic waves, plus analysis of rocks that appear on the surface, of volcanic lava, of surveys, of laboratory experiments and meteorites have made it possible to determine that, structurally, the Earth is divided into different layers.

crust ■
The outermost and thinnest layer; it is composed of sedimentary, granitic and basaltic rock

lithosphere ■
Encompasses all of the crust and the upper part of the mantle, forming plates that "float" on top of the asthenosphere

asthenosphere ■
A viscous layer located in the upper mantle upon which 'floats' the lithosphere

outer core ■
Composed of molten nickel and iron

inner core ■
Formed of solid nickel and iron

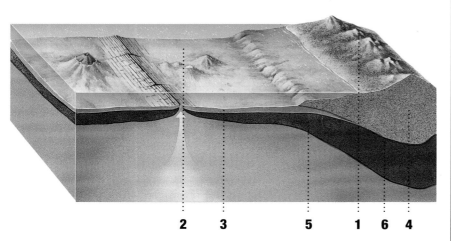

2   3   5   1   6   4

1 continental crust
20 to 50 kilometres thick; it consists of a sedimentary, a granitic and a basaltic layer

2 oceanic crust
Is characterised by the absence of the granitic layer; it has a maximum thickness of six kilometres

3 sedimentary layer
Is found in the continents and the continental platforms

4 granitic layer
Makes up the fundamental mass of the continental zones

5 basaltic layer
Is found in both continental and oceanic zones

6 Conrad discontinuity
Separates the granitic and basaltic layers of the crust

The crust's structure

The crust is not a uniform layer; instead, its composition and thickness varies according to whether it forms the oceanic or continental crust.

Wiechert-Lehmann discontinuity ■
Divides the inner from the outer core

Gutenberg discontinuity ■
Separates the lower mantle from the outer core

Repetti discontinuity ■
Divides the upper from the lower mantle

Mohorovicic discontinuity ■
Separates the crust from the mantle

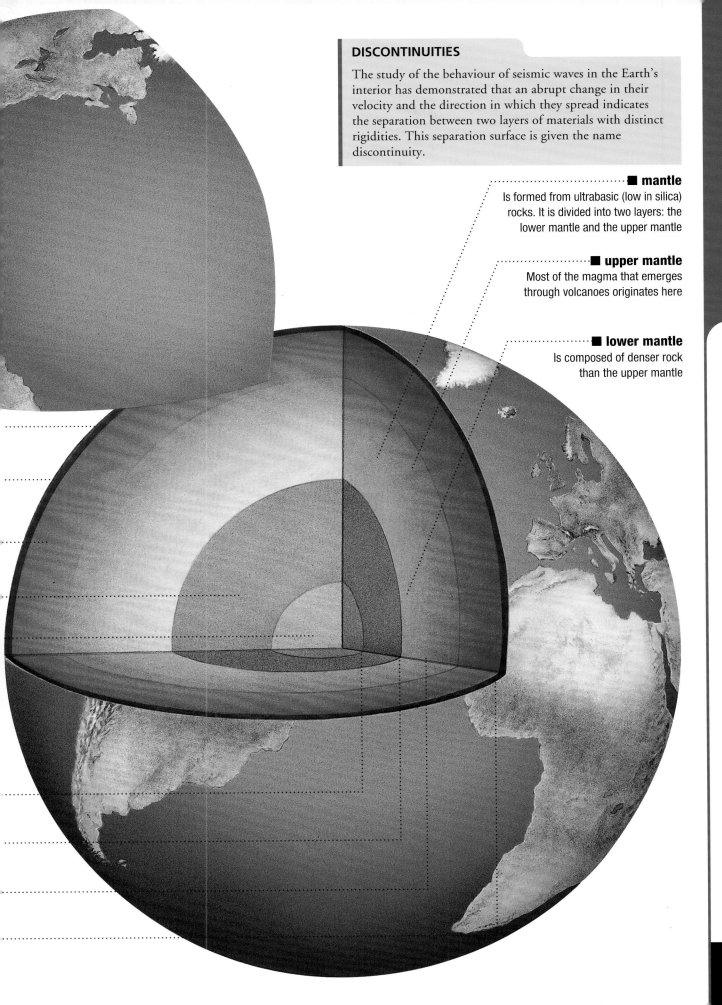

DISCONTINUITIES

The study of the behaviour of seismic waves in the Earth's interior has demonstrated that an abrupt change in their velocity and the direction in which they spread indicates the separation between two layers of materials with distinct rigidities. This separation surface is given the name discontinuity.

■ mantle
Is formed from ultrabasic (low in silica) rocks. It is divided into two layers: the lower mantle and the upper mantle

■ upper mantle
Most of the magma that emerges through volcanoes originates here

■ lower mantle
Is composed of denser rock than the upper mantle

THE GAS WE BREATHE

The atmosphere is the gaseous layer that envelops the Earth. It is principally made up of nitrogen (78%), oxygen (21%) and much lower quantities of other gases such as CO_2 and water vapour. The air is essential for life as it permits us to breathe, protects us by impeding the entry of dangerous ultraviolet radiation from the Sun and prevents the surface of the planet from being too hot or too cold. The atmosphere stays connected to the Earth thanks to the force of gravity and contains a series of distinct layers.

THE OZONE LAYER

Is found in the stratosphere, approximately 15 to 50 kilometres above the planet's surface. Ozone is an unstable compound of three oxygen atoms (O_3), which acts as a powerful solar filter that stops the passage of a small part of ultraviolet radiation, which is lethal for life on Earth.

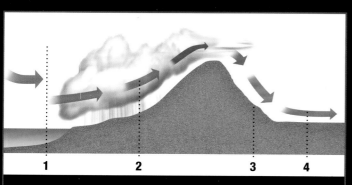

1 Hot damp air
2 Damp windward slopes
3 Dry leeward slopes
4 Dry wind (chinook)

Cloud formation

Air cools when it rises and the water vapour it contains condenses and forms small drops of water in suspension that we call clouds. Various mechanisms enable this to happen.

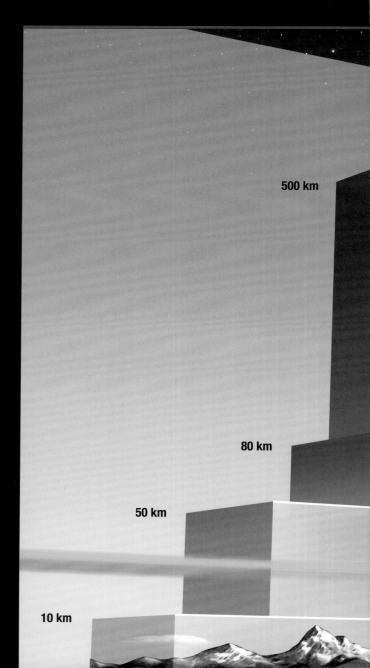

500 km

80 km

50 km

10 km

The densest layer; meteorological phenomena occur here and its composition permits the development of life.

2 tropopause
The boundary between the troposphere and the stratosphere.

3 stratosphere
Absorbtion of ultraviolet radiation takes place here thanks to the ozone layer's existence.

4 stratopause
The boundary between the stratosphere and the mesosphere.

Air density is very low here, although the proportions of its components are the same as in the troposphere; meteorites destroy themselves when they collide with this layer.

6 mesopause
Marks the boundary between the mesosphere and the thermosphere.

7 thermosphere
Air density is very low and the few atoms it contains are ionised; the Aurora Borealis arise here and it's the zone where satellites orbit.

8 ionosphere
It is not a separate layer, but it forms

radio communication is possible because different regions of the ionosphere reflect radio waves back to the Earth.

9 thermopause
The boundary between the thermosphere and the exosphere.

10 exosphere
The lightest gases escape the Earth's gravitational pull and disperse into space: they can be detected as far as 8,000 kilometres from Earth.

11 temperature
This scale shows the approximate temperature found in each atmospheric zone.

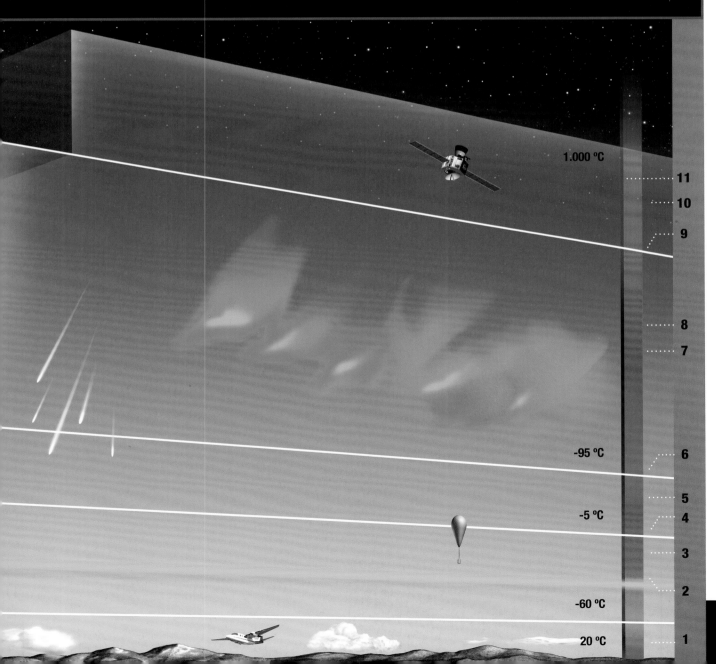

1.000 ºC

11
10
9

8
7

-95 ºC — 6

5
-5 ºC — 4

3

2

-60 ºC

20 ºC — 1

DRIFTING CONTINENTS

The crust, together with the upper mantle, makes up the lithosphere. This is not a continuous layer; instead it is broken into vast pieces called tectonic plates, which move around in relation to each other, 'floating' on the underlying, viscous layer, known as the asthenosphere. The plates' margins are unstable zones of great tectonic, seismic and volcanic activity and it is here that the terrestrial crust is created or destroyed.

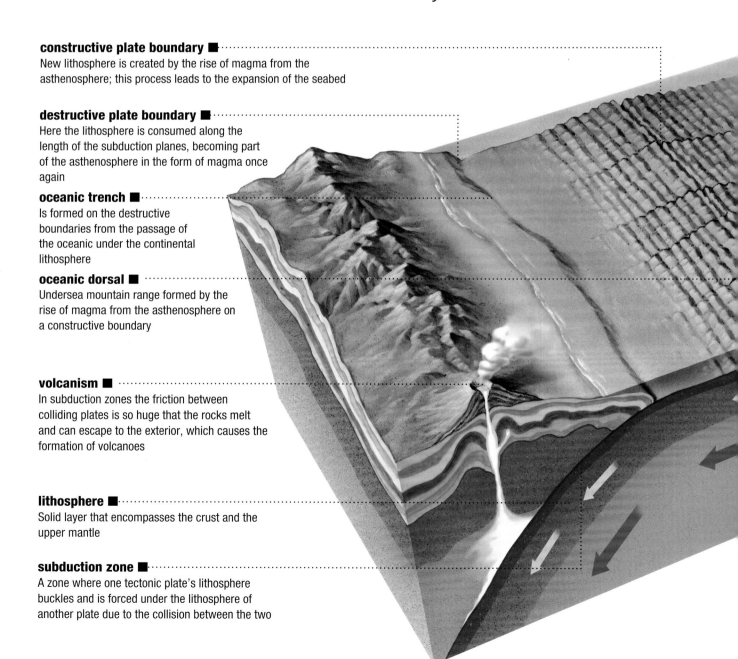

constructive plate boundary ■
New lithosphere is created by the rise of magma from the asthenosphere; this process leads to the expansion of the seabed

destructive plate boundary ■
Here the lithosphere is consumed along the length of the subduction planes, becoming part of the asthenosphere in the form of magma once again

oceanic trench ■
Is formed on the destructive boundaries from the passage of the oceanic under the continental lithosphere

oceanic dorsal ■
Undersea mountain range formed by the rise of magma from the asthenosphere on a constructive boundary

volcanism ■
In subduction zones the friction between colliding plates is so huge that the rocks melt and can escape to the exterior, which causes the formation of volcanoes

lithosphere ■
Solid layer that encompasses the crust and the upper mantle

subduction zone ■
A zone where one tectonic plate's lithosphere buckles and is forced under the lithosphere of another plate due to the collision between the two

obduction ■
Happens when two continental plates collide, deforming and compressing until they joint together in a single mass

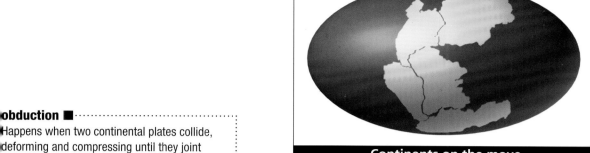

Continents on the move

At the end of the Paleozoic era, all the continents were united in a single landmass called Pangaea, around which was a single ocean called Panthalassa. Since then the crust has fractured into several plates that will finally end up reuniting once again

■ passive plate margin
Here, lithosphere is neither created nor destroyed; it normally goes with transform faults

■ asthenosphere
Viscous layer of the upper mantle upon which the lithosphere 'floats'

■ transform fault
A fracture zone that forms the margin of two plates, which slide laterally against each other; this movement often causes earthquakes

SEABEDS EXPAND

At the margins of constructive plates, matter from the upper mantle flows towards the terrestrial crust. In this way, the intruding material generates new oceanic lithosphere, and the seabed expands on both sides of ocean ridges: this causes continental drift.

■ folding
When two continental lithosphere plates collide, both masses deform and compress, giving rise to great mountain ranges

WHEN THE EARTH 'SPITS' FIRE

Volcanoes form when molten matter and gases from the Earth's interior rise to the surface through fissures. This can happen in both violent form or as a slow lava flow. Worldwide, 1,415 volcanoes have been active over the last 10,000 years. Some of them, such as the ones in Hawaii and Indonesia, or Mount Etna and Mount Stromboli, erupt frequently while others remain dormant for many years.

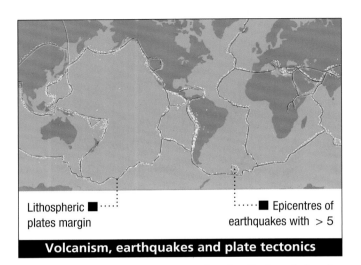

Lithospheric ■ plates margin

■ Epicentres of earthquakes with > 5

Volcanism, earthquakes and plate tectonics

Most earthquakes and volcanoes are found on the boundaries of lithospheric plates. The Pacific Ring of Fire is one of the most active zones.

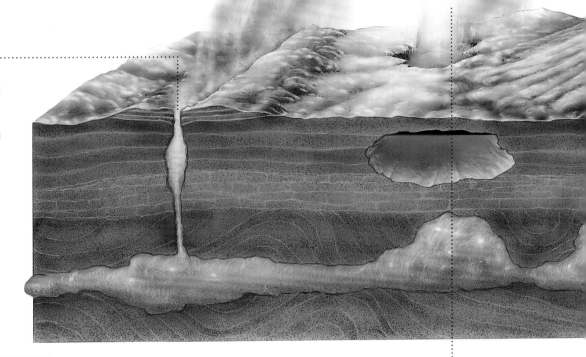

fissure volcano ■
Sometimes lava takes advantage of fissures in the terrestrial crust and flows in vast quantities along their entire length

■ **geyse**
Intermittent eruptions of boiling water; they are true wate volcanoes that occur whe underground water comes int contact with magm

THE KILLER VOLCANO

In August 1883, the volcano Krakatoa, near the island of Java, Indonesia, erupted, hurling rocks to an altitude of 55 kilometres. The island on which the volcano is located exploded with the force of 100 megatonnes (the atom bomb dropped on Hiroshima in Japan was approximately 20 megatonnes); the blast was heard in Australia and generated a 40-metre-high tsunami, or giant wave. Some 36,000 people were killed by this natural disaster.

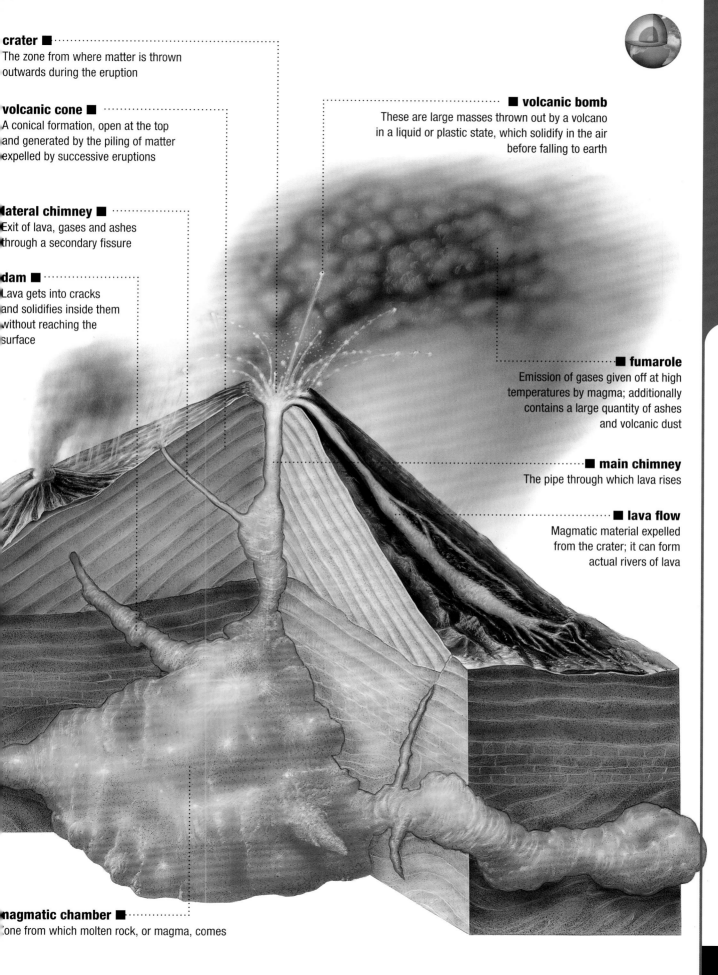

crater ■
The zone from where matter is thrown outwards during the eruption

volcanic cone ■
A conical formation, open at the top and generated by the piling of matter expelled by successive eruptions

lateral chimney ■
Exit of lava, gases and ashes through a secondary fissure

dam ■
Lava gets into cracks and solidifies inside them without reaching the surface

■ **volcanic bomb**
These are large masses thrown out by a volcano in a liquid or plastic state, which solidify in the air before falling to earth

■ **fumarole**
Emission of gases given off at high temperatures by magma; additionally contains a large quantity of ashes and volcanic dust

■ **main chimney**
The pipe through which lava rises

■ **lava flow**
Magmatic material expelled from the crater; it can form actual rivers of lava

magmatic chamber ■
Zone from which molten rock, or magma, comes

THE SUBTERRANEAN WORLD

Karstic modelling is the result of the dissolving of limestone by the action of rainwater and carbon dioxide. Although compacted, limestone can have an uneven surface, with fissures and bedding planes that give it the character of permeable rock. Run-off water penetrates via the uneven surface, attacking the limestone and then separating out part of the dissolved calcium carbonate.

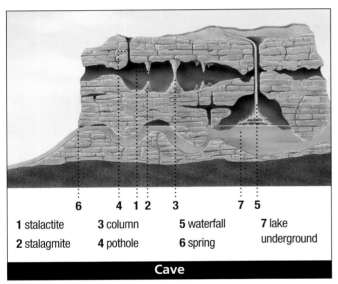

6	4 1 2	3	7 5
1 stalactite	**3** column	**5** waterfall	**7** lake underground
2 stalagmite	**4** pothole	**6** spring	

Cave

Caves are galleries widened by the fall of parts of the roof. Not only does the dissolving of limestone happen in them, but also its precipitation, giving rise to strange forms of great beauty.

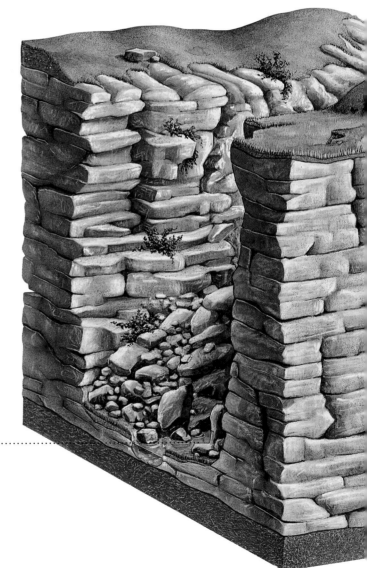

spring ■
A place where underground water flows up to the surface

underground river ■
Water uses the galleries and runs through them like an actual underground river

THE WORLD'S BIGGEST CAVE

Is found in Sarawak (Malaysia). It is 162,700 square metres in size, 700 metres long, 300 metres wide on average and, at the lowest point, 70 metres high.

■ gallery
Carved gallery normally following the surfaces that separate rock strata

■ joint
Extended crack, perpendicular to the rock stratification, which appears in family formation, all pointing in the same direction

■ pothole
Vertical hole with a funnel form that comes from the enlargement of vertical cracks

■ stalactite
Cylindrically shaped calcareous deposit that hangs from cavern roofs; formed by drops that drip from rock fissures

■ cave
Cavity formed by the widening of galleries after the falling of blocks of the roof

■ doline
Also known as a funnel cave; these are small oval-shaped depressions surrounded by vertical walls and a bottom covered in red clay

stalagmite ■
Calcareous deposit in irregular pillar shape which has grown vertically from the ground of a cavern due to calcite precipitation from drops that fall from the ceiling or from a stalactite

■ column
Forms when a stalactite and stalagmite join together

■ sump
U-shaped karstic gallery, which permits water springs to spout intermittently

RIVERS OF ICE

Glaciers are huge moving pieces of ice that form in polar regions and high mountains above the snowline. They are impressive phenomena, capable of grinding rock into dust and transporting millions of tonnes of sediment across great distances. To make them, a large quantity of snow has to accumulate and compact, and there must be a gradient steep enough so that it slides down a mountainside.

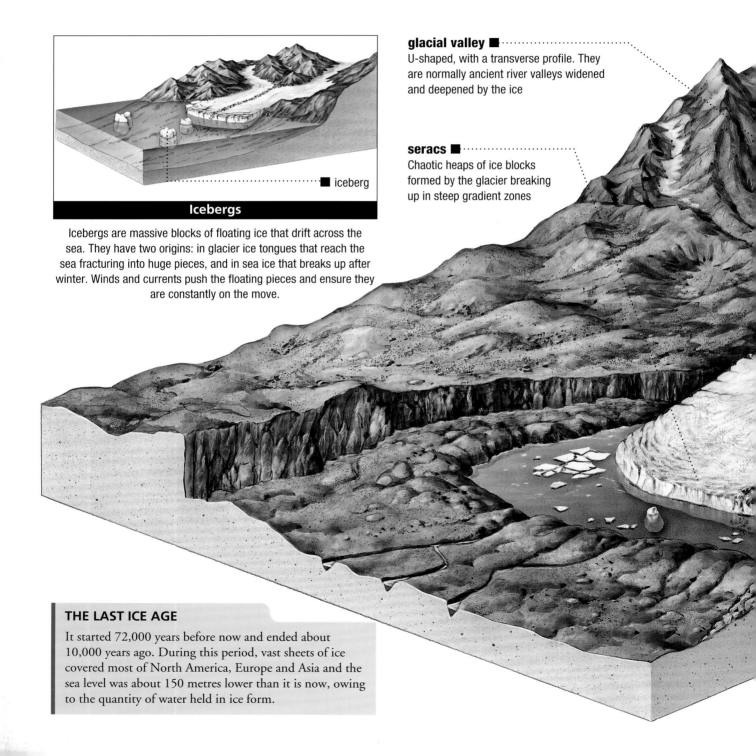

glacial valley ■
U-shaped, with a transverse profile. They are normally ancient river valleys widened and deepened by the ice

seracs ■
Chaotic heaps of ice blocks formed by the glacier breaking up in steep gradient zones

■ iceberg

Icebergs

Icebergs are massive blocks of floating ice that drift across the sea. They have two origins: in glacier ice tongues that reach the sea fracturing into huge pieces, and in sea ice that breaks up after winter. Winds and currents push the floating pieces and ensure they are constantly on the move.

THE LAST ICE AGE

It started 72,000 years before now and ended about 10,000 years ago. During this period, vast sheets of ice covered most of North America, Europe and Asia and the sea level was about 150 metres lower than it is now, owing to the quantity of water held in ice form.

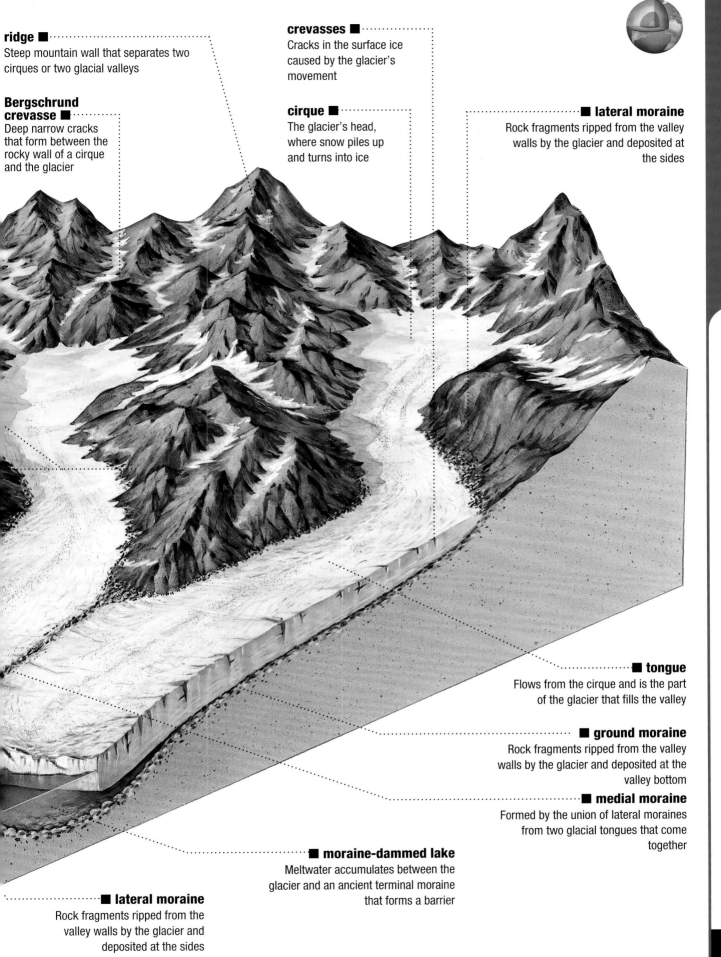

ridge ■
Steep mountain wall that separates two cirques or two glacial valleys

crevasses ■
Cracks in the surface ice caused by the glacier's movement

Bergschrund crevasse ■
Deep narrow cracks that form between the rocky wall of a cirque and the glacier

cirque ■
The glacier's head, where snow piles up and turns into ice

■ **lateral moraine**
Rock fragments ripped from the valley walls by the glacier and deposited at the sides

■ **tongue**
Flows from the cirque and is the part of the glacier that fills the valley

■ **ground moraine**
Rock fragments ripped from the valley walls by the glacier and deposited at the valley bottom

■ **medial moraine**
Formed by the union of lateral moraines from two glacial tongues that come together

■ **moraine-dammed lake**
Meltwater accumulates between the glacier and an ancient terminal moraine that forms a barrier

■ **lateral moraine**
Rock fragments ripped from the valley walls by the glacier and deposited at the sides

AN UNDERWATER WORLD

Most of the Earth is covered in water, almost all of which belongs to the seas and oceans. Due to their vast extent and depth, several distinct zones can be delineated, some of them largely unexplored and as hostile as outer space. The seabed is as varied as dry land and there we find mountain ranges, volcanoes, ravines and other features of mountain geography (orography).

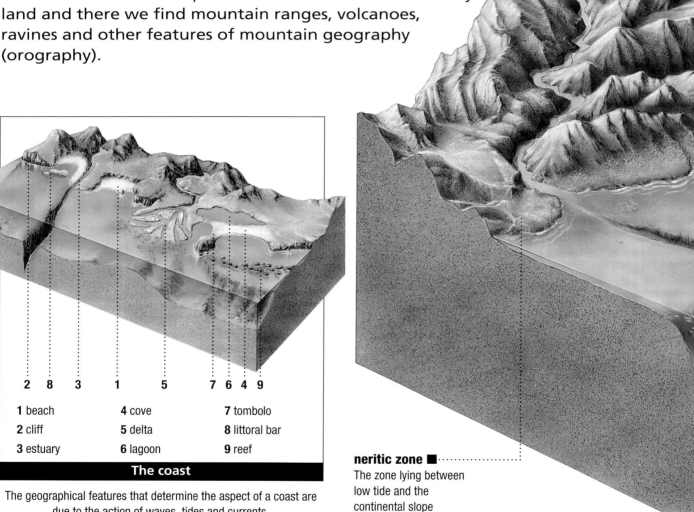

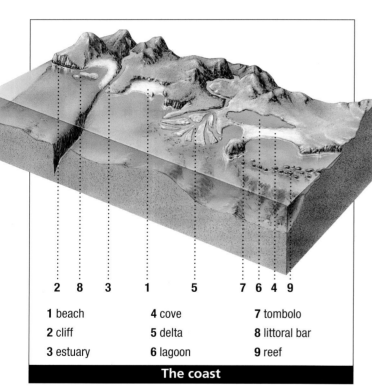

2 8 3 1 5 7 6 4 9		

1 beach	**4** cove	**7** tombolo
2 cliff	**5** delta	**8** littoral bar
3 estuary	**6** lagoon	**9** reef

The coast

The geographical features that determine the aspect of a coast are due to the action of waves, tides and currents.

neritic zone ■
The zone lying between low tide and the continental slope

undersea canyon ■
Ancient fluvial valley submerged and excavated by mud currents that happen here

THE TIDES

Tides are increases and decreases in seawater level that occur every 12 hours and 26 minutes, due mainly to the Moon and the Sun's gravitational pull on the sea's liquid mass. The maximum level is known as high tide, and the minimum, low tide.

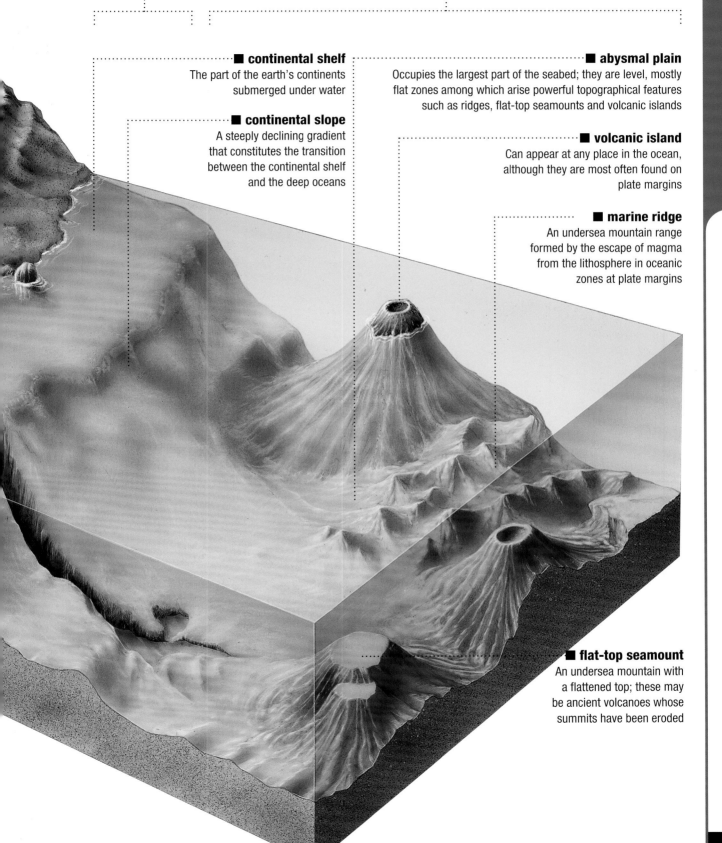

neritic zone
The zone lying between low tide and the continental slope

pelagic zone
Extends from the edge of the continental shelf and includes the deepest zones

■ **continental shelf**
The part of the earth's continents submerged under water

■ **continental slope**
A steeply declining gradient that constitutes the transition between the continental shelf and the deep oceans

■ **abysmal plain**
Occupies the largest part of the seabed; they are level, mostly flat zones among which arise powerful topographical features such as ridges, flat-top seamounts and volcanic islands

■ **volcanic island**
Can appear at any place in the ocean, although they are most often found on plate margins

■ **marine ridge**
An undersea mountain range formed by the escape of magma from the lithosphere in oceanic zones at plate margins

■ **flat-top seamount**
An undersea mountain with a flattened top; these may be ancient volcanoes whose summits have been eroded

A PLANET IN FLUX

The Earth undergoes a continuous process of transformation as a result of the combined action of opposing forces that are brought to bear on the planet's crust: one constructive and internal, the other destructive and external. These same processes have been occurring for hundreds of millions of years. The internal forces manifest themselves in the form of volcanoes, earthquakes, strata deformations, subsidence, etc. while the most obvious effect of the external forces is erosion.

- 1
- 2
- 3
- 4

1 soil horizon A
Rich in organic material, this is where vegetation takes root

2 soil horizon B
Organic material is almost completely absent; here substances dragged down from above are deposited

3 soil horizon C
Formed by weathered bedrock fragments

4 bedrock
Rock in pure form; marks the ground's lower limit

Ground

The continental crust's uppermost layer, formed by the products of the breakdown of rocks as well as air, water, organic material and living things.

THE ACTION OF LIVING THINGS

Plant roots help to widen cracks in rocks and split them, which facilitates the penetration of water and air, which also boosts chemical weathering. But it is human beings who alter the ground most rapidly when they build roads and reservoirs, dig mines, chop down woods, etc.

sedimentation ■
Transported matter is deposited in the lowest zones of the Earth's crust

weathering ■
Matter is changed by chemical acti◼ of water and air (oxidation, dissolvir hydration, hydrolysis ...)

subsidence ■
Constant sedimentation increases the weight and this leads to a sinking of sediments

metamorphism ■
Increases in pressure and temperature in the rock lead to mineralogical changes that produce another type of rock called metamorphic rock

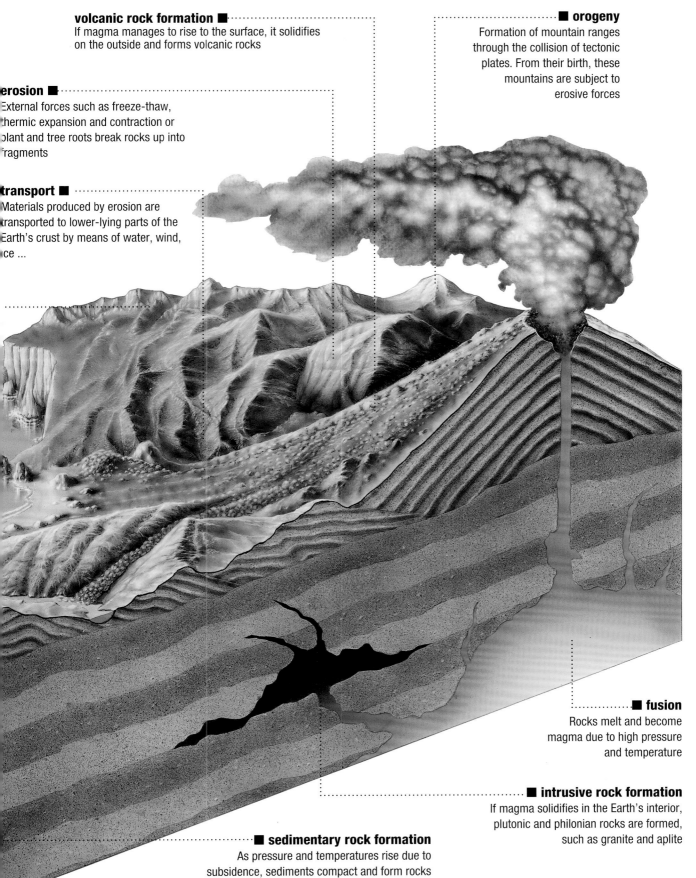

volcanic rock formation ■
If magma manages to rise to the surface, it solidifies on the outside and forms volcanic rocks

erosion ■
External forces such as freeze-thaw, thermic expansion and contraction or plant and tree roots break rocks up into fragments

transport ■
Materials produced by erosion are transported to lower-lying parts of the Earth's crust by means of water, wind, ice ...

■ orogeny
Formation of mountain ranges through the collision of tectonic plates. From their birth, these mountains are subject to erosive forces

■ fusion
Rocks melt and become magma due to high pressure and temperature

■ intrusive rock formation
If magma solidifies in the Earth's interior, plutonic and philonian rocks are formed, such as granite and aplite

■ sedimentary rock formation
As pressure and temperatures rise due to subsidence, sediments compact and form rocks

A SPHERE REPRESENTED ON A FLAT PLANE

A map is a two-dimensional (length and width) representation of an area, but the Earth and all of its topographical features have three dimensions, so the third dimension (height) is represented through contours. These contours are lines that unite topographic points located at the same height above sea level. In order to represent an area on a flat plane, it is assumed that the topographic point is intersected by a series of equidistant levels, whose projection on a plane gives the outline of the contours.

4 escarpment ■

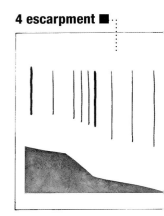

3 steep gradient ■

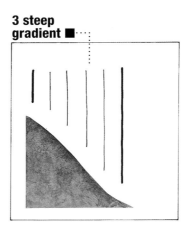

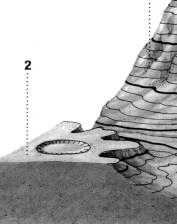

2 plateau ■

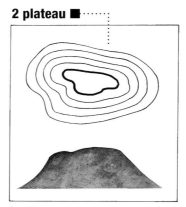

1 valley ■

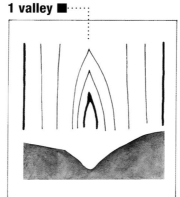

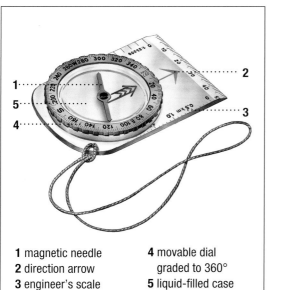

1 magnetic needle
2 direction arrow
3 engineer's scale
4 movable dial graded to 360°
5 liquid-filled case

The compass

This instrument features a needle that orients itself using the lines of force of the Earth's magnetic field and points us in the direction of terrestrial magnetic north.

WHERE IS NORTH?

There are three versions of north: geographic north (which is the intersection point bvetween the Earth's rotational axis and its surface), magnetic north (which is what the compass shows) and the third north (which is what the map shows). The difference between the first two is called magnetic declination and its value depends on the time period and our location.

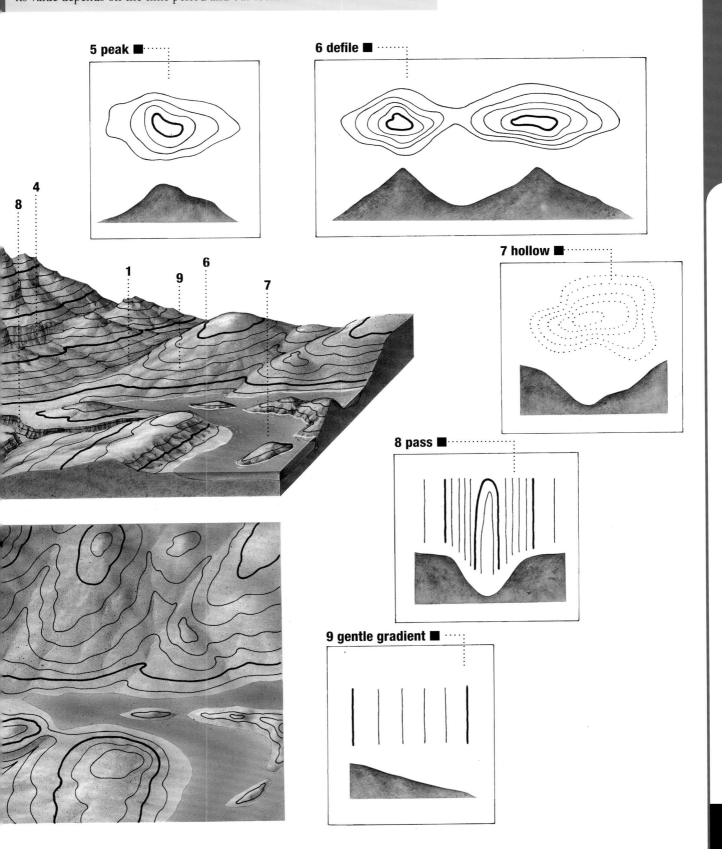

5 peak ■

6 defile ■

7 hollow ■

8 pass ■

9 gentle gradient ■

FIND OUT MORE

Era		Period	Characteristic fauna		Myr*
Phanerozoic	Cenozoic	Quaternary	Current fauna	Human era	
			Primitive hominids		
			Mammoths		1,8
		Neogene	Mammals	Mammal era	
			Bivalve molluscs		
			Lacustrine snails		23,8
		Paleogene	Nummulites		
			Mammals		
			Echinoderms (sea urchins)		65
	Mesozoic	Cretaceous	Ammonites	Reptile and ammonite era	
			Foraminifera		
			Dinosaurs		
			Pachydonts		144
		Jurassic	Ammonites		
			Belemnites		
			Reptiles		
			Toothed birds		206
		Triassic	Ammonites		
			Bivalve molluscs		
			Crinoids		
			Reptiles (dinosaurs)		248
	Paleozoic	Permian	Amphibians	Trilobyte era	
			First reptiles		
			Brachiopods		290
		Carboniferous	Goniatites		
			Brachiopods		
			Fusulinidas		
			Amphibians		360
		Devonian	Armoured fish		
			Ostracodes		
			Goniatids		
			Corals		
			Brachiopods		409

Era		Period	Characteristic fauna		Myr*
Phanerozoic	Paleozoic	Silurian	Graptolites	Trilobyte era	
			Conodonts		439
		Ordovician	Graptolites		
			Brachiopods		
			Gastropods		510
		Cambrian	Trilobites		
			Brachiopods		
			Archaeocyathids (calcareous sponges)		570
	Precambrian	Protozoic	Invertebrates with no rigid skeletons		
			First multicellular algae		
			First protozoa		
			First multicellular organisms		2.500
		Archean	First eukaryotic cells (bacteria)		3.900
		Hadean			4.600

* Millions of years

GEOLOGICAL PERIODS

Geological processes, in general, happen so slowly that they are beyond the possibilities of human observation. For this reason, geologists have developed a timescale, based on global geological and biological events, which is used as an absolute temporal frame of reference. It takes the Earth's formation as its starting point, although it counts backwards in millions of years. Its time periods are established using geological (stratigraphic) and biological criteria. The major periods have a planetary reach and are the fundamentals of establishing geological time.

THE EARTH IN NUMBERS

Mass (kg)	$5{,}97 \cdot 10^{24}$
Equatorial radius (km)	6.378,14
Average density (g/cm³)	5,515
Average distance to the Sun (km)	149.600.000
Rotational period (days)	0,99727
Rotational period (hours)	23,9345
Orbital period (days)	365,256
Average orbital velocity (km/sec)	29,79
Axis incline	23,450°
Average equatorial surface gravity (m/sec²)	9,78
Temperature	-89 °C - 58 °C
Average surface temperature	15 °C
Atmospheric pressure (bars)	1,013
Atmospheric composition	
Nitrogen	77 %
Oxygen	21 %
Others	2 %

EARTHQUAKES

Earthquakes occur when pressure built up by the deformation of the Earth's layers is abruptly released. Rocks shatter as they are subjected to gigantic forces, reordering matter and releasing an immense energy that shakes the Earth. Starting points (epicentres) are found at different depths - the deepest can go as far as 700 kilometres beneath the Earth's surface. They are especially frequent along the boundaries of the tectonic plates. These tremors are very difficult to predict and currently there are no efficient systems for alerting the population to the imminence of a seismic shock ahead of time.

COMPARATIVE TABLE OF THE MERCALLI AND RICHTER SCALES

Mercalli Scale (magnitude)	Richter Scale (intensity)	Observations
I	Up to 2.5 instrumental	Weak earthquake only recorded by seismographs.
II	2.5-3.1 very weak	Felt only by resting people.
III	3.1-3.7 light	Felt in densely populated areas by a section of the population.
IV	3.7-4.3 moderate	Felt by people on the move, some people asleep are woken up.
V	4.3-4.9 quite strong	Felt outside, wakes people up.
VI	4.9-5.5 strong	Felt by all, walking unstable, trees and objects shake because of the earthquake's effect.
VII	5.5-6.1 very strong	Difficult to stay standing, suspended objects fall, minor structural collapse and landslips possible.
VIII	6.1-6.7 destructive	Partial collapse of structures, considerable damage to ordinary buildings.
IX	6.7-7.3 ruinous	Considerable damage to reinforced structures, complete collapse of buildings and houses, general damage to foundations, dams and dykes.
X	7.3-7.9 disastrous	Destruction of the majority of buildings, toppling of bridges, serious damage to dams and jetties.
XI	7.9-8.4 very disastrous	Few structures remain standing, huge fissures in the ground.
XII	8.4-9 catastrophic	Total destruction, vast quantities of displaced rock, objects tossed into the air.